ANARCHY

Errico Malatesta

ISBN: 978-1505679397

www.dogstailbooks.co.uk

ANARCHY is a word which comes from the Greek, and signifies, strictly speaking, *without government:* the state of a people without any constituted authority, that is, without government.

Before such an organization had begun to be considered possible and desirable by a whole class of thinkers, so as to be taken as the aim of a party (which party has now become one of the most important factors in modern social warfare), the word Anarchy was taken universally in the sense of disorder and confusion; and it is still adopted in that sense by the ignorant and by adversaries interested in distorting the truth.

We shall not enter into philological discussions; for the question is not philological but historical. The common meaning of the word does not misconceive its true etymological signification, but is derived from this meaning, owing to the prejudice that government must be a necessity of the organization of social life; and that consequently a society without government must be given up to disorder, and oscillate between the unbridled dominion of some and the blind vengeance of others.

The existence of this prejudice, and its influence on the meaning which the public has given the word, is easily explained.

Man, like all living beings, adapts and habituates himself to the conditions in which he lives, and transmits by inheritance his acquired habits. Thus being born and having lived in bondage, being the descendant of a long line of slaves, man, when he began to think, believed that slavery was an essential condition of life; and liberty seemed to him an impossible thing. In like manner, the workman, forced for centuries, and thus habituated, to depend upon the good will of his employer for work, that is, for bread, and accustomed to see his own life at the disposal of those who possess the land and the capital, has ended in believing that it is his master who gives him to eat, and demands ingenuously how it would be possible to live, if there were no master over him?

In the same way, a man who had had his limbs bound from his birth, but had nevertheless found out how to hobble about, might attribute to the very hands that bound him his ability to move, while, on the contrary, they would be diminishing and paralyzing the muscular energy of his limbs.

If, then, we add to the natural effect of habit the education given him by his masters, the parson, teacher, etc., who are all interested in teaching that the employer and the government are necessary; if also we add the judge and the bailiff to force those who think differently-- and might try to propagate their opinions --to keep silence, we shall understand how the prejudice as to the utility and necessity of masters and governments has become established. Suppose a doctor brings forward a complete theory, with a thousand ably invented illustrations, to persuade that man with the bound limb whom we were describing, that, if his limb were freed, he could not walk, could not even live. The man would defend his bands furiously, and consider any one his enemy who tried to tear them off.

Thus, since it is believed that government is necessary, and that without government there must be disorder and confusion, it is natural and logical to suppose that Anarchy, which signifies without government, must also mean absence of order.

Nor is this fact without parallel in the history of words. In those epochs and countries where people have considered government by one man (monarchy) necessary, the word republic (that is, the government of many) has been used precisely like Anarchy, to imply disorder and confusion. Traces of this signification of the word are still to be found in the popular language of almost all countries.

When this opinion is changed, and the public convinced that government is not necessary, but extremely harmful, the word Anarchy, precisely because it signifies without government, will become equal to saying natural order, harmony of the needs and interests of all, complete liberty with complete solidarity.

Therefore, those are wrong who say that Anarchists have chosen their name badly, because it is erroneously understood by the masses and leads to a false interpretation. The error does not come from the word, but from the thing. The difficulty which Anarchists meet with in spreading their views does not depend upon the name they have given themselves, but upon the fact that their conceptions strike at all the inveterate prejudices that people have about the function of government, or the *State*, as it is called.

Before proceeding further, it will be well to explain this last word (the State) which, in our opinion, is the real cause of much misunderstanding.

Anarchists, and we among them, have made use, and still generally make use of the word State, meaning thereby that collection of institutions, political, legislative, judicial, military, financial, etc., by means of which the management of their own affairs, the guidance of their personal conduct and the care of ensuring their own safety are taken from the people and confided to certain individuals. And these, whether by usurpation or delegation, are invested with the right to make laws over and for all, and to constrain the public to respect them, making use of the collective force of the community to this end.

In this case the word State means government, or, if you like, it is the impersonal expression, abstracted from the state of things, of which the government is the personification. Then such expressions as abolition of the State, or society without the State, agree perfectly with the conception which Anarchists wish to express of the destruction of every political institution based on authority, and of the constitution of a free and equal society, based upon harmony of interests, and the voluntary contribution of all to the satisfaction of social needs.

However, the word State has many other significations, and among these some which lend themselves to misconstruction, particularly when used among men whose sad social position has not afforded them leisure to become accustomed to the delicate distinctions of scientific language, or, still worse, when adopted treacherously by adversaries, who are interested in confounding the sense, or do not wish to comprehend. Thus the word State is often used to indicate any given society, or collection of human beings, united on a given territory and constituting what is called a social unit, independently of the way in which the members of the said body are grouped, or of the relations existing between them. State is used also simply as a synonym for society. Owing to these significations of the word, our adversaries believe, or rather profess to believe, that Anarchists wish to abolish every social relation and all collective work, and to reduce man to a condition of isolation, that is, to a state worse than savagery.

By State again is meant only the supreme administration of a country, the central power, distinct from provincial or communal power; and therefore others think that Anarchists wish merely for a territorial decentralization, leaving the principle of government intact, and thus confounding Anarchy with cantonal or communal government.

Finally, state signifies condition, mode of living, the order of social life, etc., and therefore we say, for example, that it is necessary to change the economic state of the working classes, or that the Anarchical state is the only state founded on the principles of solidarity, and other similar phrases. So that if we say also in another sense that we wish to abolish the State, we may at once appear absurd or contradictory.

For these reasons, we believe it would be better to use the expression *abolition of the State* as little as possible, and to substitute for it another clearer and more concrete--*abolition of government.*

In any case, the latter will be the expression used in the course of this little work.

We have said that Anarchy is society without government. But is the suppression of government possible, desirable, or wise? Let us see.

What is the government? There is a disease of the human mind called the metaphysical tendency, causing man, after he has by a logical process abstracted the quality from an object, to be subject to a kind of hallucination which makes him take the abstraction for the real thing. This metaphysical tendency, in spite of the blows of positive science, has still strong root in the minds of the majority of our contemporary fellow men. It has such an influence that many consider government an actual entity, with certain given attributes of reason, justice, equity, independently of the people who compose the government.

For those who think in this way, government, or the State, is the abstract social power, and it represents, always in the abstract, the general interest. It is the expression of the right of all, and considered as limited by the rights of each. This way of understanding government

6

is supported by those interested, to whom it is an urgent necessity that the principle of authority should be maintained, and should always survive the faults and errors of the persons who succeed to the exercise of power.

For us, the government is the aggregate of the governors; and the governors--kings, presidents, ministers, members of parliament, and what not--are those who have the power to make laws, to regulate the relations between men, and to force obedience to these laws. They are those who decide upon and claim the taxes, enforce military service, judge and punish transgressions of the laws. They subject men to regulations, and supervise and sanction private contracts. They monopolize certain branches of production and public services, or, if they wish, all production and public service. They promote or hinder the exchange of goods. They make war or peace with the governments of other countries. They concede or withhold free trade and many things else. In short, the governors are those who have the power, in a greater or less degree, to make use of the collective force of society, that is, of the physical, intellectual, and economic force of all, to oblige each to do the said governor's wish. And this power constitutes, in our opinion, the very principle of government, the principle of authority.

But what reason is there for the existence of government?

Why abdicate one's own liberty, one's own initiative in favor of other individuals? Why give them the power to be the masters, with or contrary to the wish of each, to dispose of the forces of all in their own way? Are the governors such very exceptionally gifted men as to enable them, with some show of reason, to represent the masses, and act in the interest of all men better than all men would be able to do for themselves? Are they so infallible and incorruptible that one can confide to them, with any semblance of prudence, the fate of each and all, trusting to their knowledge and their goodness?

And even if there existed men of infinite goodness and knowledge, even if we assume what has never been verified in history, and what we believe it would be impossible to verify, namely, that the government might devolve upon the ablest and best, would the possession of governmental power add anything to their beneficent influence? Would it not rather paralyze or destroy it? For those who govern find it necessary to occupy themselves with things which they do not understand, and, above all, to waste the greater part of their energy in keeping themselves in power, striving to satisfy their friends, holding the discontented in check, and mastering the rebellious.

Again, be the governors good or bad, wise or ignorant, who is it that appoints them to their office? Do they impose themselves by right of war, conquest, or revolution? Then, what guarantees have the public that their rulers have the general good at heart? In this case it is simply a question of usurpation; and if the subjects are discontented, nothing is left to them but to throw off the yoke, by an appeal to arms. Are the governors chosen from a certain class or party? Then certainly the ideas and interests of that class or party will triumph, and the wishes and interests of the others will be sacrificed. Are they elected by universal suffrage? Now numbers are the sole criterion; and numbers are certainly no proof of reason, justice or capacity. Under universal suffrage, the elected are those who know best how to take in the masses. The minority, which may happen to be half minus one, is sacrificed. And that without considering that there is another thing to take into account.

Experience has shown it is impossible to hit upon an electoral system which really ensures election by the actual majority.

Many and various are the theories by which men have sought to justify the existence of government. All, however, are founded, confessedly or not, on the assumption that the individuals of a society have contrary interests, and that an external superior power is necessary to oblige some to respect the interests of others, by prescribing and imposing a rule of conduct, according to which the interests at strife may be harmonized as much as possible, and according to which each obtains the maximum of satisfaction with the minimum of sacrifice. If, say the theorists of the authoritarian school, the interests, tendencies, and desires of an individual are in opposition to those of another individual, or mayhap all society, who will have the right and the power to oblige the one to respect the interests of the others? Who will be able to prevent the individual citizen from offending the general will? The liberty of each, say they, has for its limit the liberty of others; but who will establish those limits, and who will cause them to be respected? The natural antagonism of interests and passions creates the necessity for government, and justifies authority. Authority intervenes as moderator of the social strife, and defines the limits of the rights and duties of each.

This is the theory; but the theory, to be sound, ought to be based upon facts, and to explain them. We know well how in social economy theories are too often invented to justify facts, that is, to defend privilege and cause it to be accepted tranquilly by those who are its victims. Let us here look at the facts themselves.

In all the course of history, as at the present epoch, government is either the brutal, violent, arbitrary domination of the few over the many, or it is an instrument ordained to secure domination and privilege to those who, by force, or cunning, or inheritance, have taken to themselves all the means of life, and first and foremost the soil, whereby they hold the people in servitude, making them work for their advantage.

Governments oppress mankind in two ways, either directly, by brute force, that is physical violence, or indirectly, by depriving them of the means of subsistence and thus reducing them to helplessness at discretion. Political power originated in the first method; economic privilege arose from the second. Governments can also oppress man by acting on his emotional nature, and in this way constitute religious authority. But there is no reason for the propagation of religious superstitions except that they defend and consolidate political and economic privileges.

In primitive society, when the world was not so densely populated as now, and social relations were less complicated, when any circumstance prevented the formation of habits and customs of solidarity, or destroyed those which already existed, and established the domination of man over man, the two powers, the political and the economical, were united in the same hands --and often also in those of one single individual. Those who had by force conquered and impoverished the others, constrained them to become their servants, and perform all things for them according to their caprice. The victors were at once proprietors, legislators, kings, judges, and executioners.

But with the increase of population, with the growth of needs, with the complication of social relationships, the prolonged continuance of such despotism became impossible. For their own security, the rulers, often much against their will, were obliged to depend upon a privileged class, that is, a certain number of co-interested individuals, and were also obliged to let each of these individuals provide for his own sustenance. Nevertheless they reserved to themselves the supreme or ultimate control. In other words, the rulers reserved to themselves the right to exploit all at their own convenience, and so to satisfy their kingly vanity. Thus private wealth was developed under the shadow of the ruling power, for its protection and--often unconsciously--as its accomplice. Thus the class of proprietors rose. And they, concentrating little by little the means of wealth in their own hands, all the means of production, the very fountains of life--agriculture, industry, and exchange--ended by becoming a power in themselves. This power, by the superiority of its means of action, and the great mass of interests it embraces, always ends by more or less openly subjugating the political power, that is, the government, which it makes its policeman.

This phenomenon has been reproduced often in history. Every time that, by invasion or any military enterprise whatever, physical brute force has taken the upper hand in society, the conquerors have shown the tendency to concentrate government and property in their own hands. In every case, however, as the government cannot attend to the production of wealth, and overlook and direct everything, it finds it needful to conciliate a powerful class, and private property is again established. With it comes the division of the two sorts of power, that of the persons who control the collective force of society, and that of the proprietors, upon whom these governors become essentially independent, because the proprietors command the sources of the said collective force.

But never has this state of things been so accentuated as in modern times. The development of production, the immense extension of commerce, the extensive power that money has acquired, and all the economic results flowing from the discovery of America, the invention of machinery, etc., have secured such supremacy to the capitalist class that it is no longer content to trust to the support of the government, and has come to wish that the government shall emanate from itself; a government composed of members of its own class, continually under its control and especially organized to defend its class against the possible revenge of the disinherited. Hence the origin of the modern parliamentary system.

Today the government is composed of proprietors, or people of their class so entirely under their influence that the richest of them do not find it necessary to take an active part in it themselves. Rothschild, for instance, does not need to be either M.P. or minister, it is enough for him to keep M.P.'s and ministers dependent upon himself.

In many countries, the proletariat participates nominally, more or less, in the election of the government. This is a concession which the *bourgeois* (*i. e.*, proprietory) class have made, either to avail themselves of popular support in the strife against royal or aristocratic power, or to divert the attention of the people from their own emancipation by giving them an apparent share in political power. However, whether the *bourgeoisie* foresaw it or not, when first they conceded to the people the right to vote, the fact is that the right has proved in reality a mockery, serving only to consolidate the power of the *bourgeois*, while giving to the most energetic only of the proletariat the illusory hope of arriving at power.

So also with universal suffrage--we might say, especially with universal suffrage--the government has remained the servant and police of the *bourgeois* class. How could it be otherwise? If the government should reach the point of becoming hostile, if the hope of democracy should ever be more than a delusion deceiving the people, the proprietory class, menaced in its interests, would at once rebel, and would use all the force and influence which come from the possession of wealth, to reduce the government to the simple function of acting as policeman.

In all times and in all places, whatever may be the name that the government takes, whatever has been its origin, or its organization, its essential function is always that of oppressing and exploiting the masses, and of defending the oppressors and exploiters. Its principal characteristic and indispensable instruments are the bailiff and the tax collector, the soldier and the prison. And to these are necessarily added the time-serving priest or teacher, as the case may be, supported and protected by the government, to render the spirit of the people servile and make them docile under the yoke.

Certainly, in addition to this primary business, to this essential department of governmental action other departments have been added in the course of time. We even admit that never, or hardly ever, has a government been able to exist in a country that was at all civilized without adding to its oppressing and exploiting functions others useful and indispensable to social life. But this fact makes it none the less true that government is in its nature oppressive and a means of exploitation, and that its origin and position doom it to be the defence and hot-bed of a dominant class, thus confirming and increasing the evils of domination.

The government assumes the business of protecting, more or less vigilantly, the life of citizens against direct and brutal attacks; acknowledges and legalizes a certain number of rights and primitive usages and customs, without which it is impossible to live in society. It organizes and directs certain public services, as the post, preservation and construction of roads, care of the public health, benevolent institutions, workhouses and such like; and it pleases it to pose as the protector and benefactor of the poor and weak. But it is sufficient to notice how and why it fulfils these functions to prove our point. The fact is that everything the government undertakes it is always inspired with the spirit of domination, and ordained to defend, enlarge, and perpetuate the privileges of property, and those classes of which government is the representative and defender.

A government cannot rule for any length of time without hiding its true nature behind the pretence of general utility. It cannot respect the lives of the privileged without assuming the air of wishing to respect the lives of all. It cannot cause the privileges of some to be tolerated without appearing as the custodian of the rights of everybody. "The law" (and, of course, those that have made the law, that is, the government) "has utilized," says Kropotkin, "the social sentiments of man, working into them those precepts of morality, which man has accepted, together with arrangements useful to the minority--the exploiters--and opposed to the interests of those who might have rebelled, had it not been for this show of a moral ground."

A government cannot wish the destruction of the community, for then it and the dominant class could not claim their exploitation-gained wealth; nor could the government leave the community to manage its own affairs; for then the people would soon discover that it (the government) was necessary for no other end than to defend the proprietory class who impoverish them, and would hasten to rid themselves of both government and proprietory class.

Today in the face of the persistent and menacing demands of the proletariat, governments show a tendency to interfere in the relations between employers and work people. Thus they try to arrest the labor movement, and to impede with delusive reforms the attempts of the poor to take to themselves that which is due to them, namely an equal share of the good things of life which others enjoy.

We must also remember that on the one hand the bourgeois, that is, the proprietory class, make war among themselves, and destroy one another continually, and on the other hand that the government, although composed of the *bourgeois* and, acting as their servant and protector, is still, like every other servant or protector, continually striving to emancipate itself and to domineer over its charge. Thus this see-saw game, this swaying between conceding and withdrawing, this seeking allies among the people against the classes, and among the classes against the masses, forms the science of the governors, and blinds the ingenuous and phlegmatic, who are always expecting that salvation is coming to them from on high.

With all this, the government does not change its nature. If it acts as regulator or guarantor of the rights and duties of each, it perverts the sentiment of justice. It justifies wrong and punishes every act which offends or menaces the privileges of the governors and proprietors. It declares just,*legal*, the most atrocious exploitation of the miserable, which means a slow and continuous material and moral murder, perpetrated by those who have on those who have not. Again, if it administrates public services, it always considers the interests of the governors and proprietors, not occupying itself with the interests of the working masses, except in so far as is necessary to make the masses willing to endure their share of taxation. If it instructs, it fetters and curtails the truth, and tends to prepare the mind and heart of the young to become either implacable tyrants or docile slaves, according to the class to which they belong. In the hands of the government everything becomes a means of exploitation, everything serves as a police measure, useful to hold the people in check. And it must be thus. If the life of mankind consists in strife between man and man, naturally there must be conquerors and conquered; and the government, which is the prize of the strife, or is a means of securing to the victors the results of their victory, and perpetuating those results, will certainly never fall to those who have lost, whether the battle be on the grounds of physical or intellectual strength, or in the field of economics. And those who have fought to conquer, that is, to secure to themselves better conditions than others can have, to conquer privilege and add dominion to power, and have attained the victory, will certainly not use it to defend the rights of the vanquished, and to place limits to their own power and to that of their friends and partizans.

The government--or the State, if you will--as judge, moderator of social strife, impartial administrator of the public interests, is a lie. It is an illusion, a Utopia, never realized and never realizable. If in truth, the interests of men must always be contrary to one another; if indeed, the strife between mankind has made laws necessary to human society, and the liberty of the individual must be limited by the liberty of other individuals; then each one would always seek to make his interests triumph over those of others. Each would strive to enlarge his own liberty at the cost of the liberty of others, and there would be government. Not simply because it was more or less useful to the totality of the members of society to have a government, but because the conquerors would wish to secure to themselves the fruits of victory. They would wish effectually to subject the vanquished, and relieve themselves of the trouble of being always on the defensive, and they would appoint men, specially adapted to the business, to act as police. Were this indeed actually the case, then humanity would be destined to perish amidst periodical contests between the tyranny of the dominators and the rebellion of the conquered.

But fortunately the future of humanity is a happier one, because the law which governs it is milder.

This law is the law of *solidarity*.

I.

Man has two necessary fundamental characteristics, *the instinct of his own preservation*, without which no being could exist, and *the instinct of the preservation of his species*, without which no species could have been formed or have continued to exist. He is naturally driven to defend his own existence and well-being and that of his offspring against every danger.

In nature, living beings find two ways of securing their existence, and rendering it pleasanter. The one is in individual strife with the elements, and with other individuals of the same or different species; the other is *mutual support*, or *co-operation*, which might also be described as association for strife against all natural factors, destructive to existence, or to the development and well-being of the associated.

We do not need to investigate in these pages--and we cannot for lack of space--what respective proportions in the evolution of the organic world these two principles of strife and co-operation take.

It will suffice to note how co-operation among men (whether forced or voluntary) has become the sole means of progress, of improvement or of securing safety; and how strife--relic of an earlier stage of existence-- has become thoroughly unsuitable as a means of securing the well-being of individuals, and produces instead injury to all, both the conquerors and the conquered.

The accumulated and transmitted experience of successive generations has taught man that by uniting with other men his preservation is better secured and his well-being increased. Thus out of this same strife for existence, carried on against surrounding nature, and against individuals of their own species, the social instinct has been developed among men, and has completely transformed the conditions of their life. Through co-operation man has been enabled to evolve out of animalism, has risen to great power, and elevated himself to such a degree above the other animals, that metaphysical philosophers have believed it necessary to invent for him an immaterial and immortal soul.

Many concurrent causes have contributed to the formation of this social instinct, that starting from the animal basis of the instinct for the preservation of the species, has now become so extended and so intense that it constitutes the essential element of man's moral nature.

Man, however he evolved from inferior animal types, was a physically weak being, unarmed for the fight against carnivorous beasts. But he was possessed of a brain capable of great development, and a vocal organ, able to express the various cerebral vibrations, by means of diverse sounds, and hands adapted to give the desired form to matter. He must have very soon felt the need and advantages of association with his fellows. Indeed it may even be said that he could only rise out of animalism when he became social, and had acquired the use of language, which is at the same time a consequence and a potent factor of sociability.

The relatively scanty number of the human species rendered the strife for existence between man and man, even beyond the limits of association, less sharp, less continuous, and less necessary. At the same time, it must have greatly favored the development of sympathetic sentiments, and have left time for the discovery and appreciation of the utility of mutual support. In short, social life became the necessary condition of man's existence, in consequence of his capacity to modify his external surroundings and adapt them to his own wants, by the exercise of his primeval power in co-operation with a greater or less number of associates. His desires have multiplied with the means of satisfying them, and have become needs. And division of labor has arisen from man's methodical use of nature for his own advantage. Therefore, as now evolved, man could not live apart from his fellows without falling back into a state of animalism. Through the refinement of sensibility, with the multiplication of social relationships, and through habit impressed on the species by hereditary transmission for thousands of centuries, this need of social life, this interchange of thought and of affection between man and man, has become a mode of being necessary for our organism. It has been transformed into sympathy, friendship and love, and subsists independently of the material advantages that association procures. So much is this the case, that man will often face suffering of every kind, and even death, for the satisfaction of these sentiments.

The fact is that a totally different character has been given to the strife for existence between man and man, and between the inferior animals, by the enormous advantages that association gives to man; by the fact that his physical powers are altogether disproportionate to his intellectual superiority over the beasts, so long as he remains isolated; by his possibility of associating with an ever increasing number of individuals, and entering into more and more intricate and complex relationships, until he reaches association with all humanity; and, finally, perhaps more than all, by his ability to produce, working in co-operation with others, more than he needs to live upon. It is evident that these causes, together with the sentiments of affection derived from them, must give quite a peculiar character to the struggle for existence among human beings.

Although it is now known--and the researches of modern naturalists bring us every day new proofs--that co-operation has played, and still plays, a most important part in the development of the organic world, nevertheless, the difference between the human struggle for existence and that of the inferior animals is enormous. It is in fact proportionate to the distance separating man from the other animals. And this is none the less true because of that Darwinian theory, which the *bourgeois* class have ridden to death, little suspecting the extent to which mutual co-operation has assisted in the development of the lower animals.

The lower animals fight either individually, or, more often, in little permanent or transitory groups, against all nature, the other individuals of their own species included. Some of the more social animals, such as ants, bees, etc., associate together in the same anthill, or beehive, but are at war with, or indifferent towards, other communities of their own species. Human strife with nature, on the contrary, tends always to broaden association among men, to unite their interests, and to develop each individual's sentiments of affection towards all others, so that united they may conquer and dominate the dangers of external nature by and for humanity.

All strife directed towards obtaining advantages independently of other men, and in opposition to them, contradicts the social nature of modern man, and tends to lead it back to a more animal condition.

Solidarity, that is, harmony of interests and sentiments, the sharing of each in the good of all, and of all in the good of each, is the state in which alone man can be true to his own nature, and attain to the highest development and happiness. It is the aim towards which human development tends. It is the one great principle, capable of reconciling all present antagonisms in society, otherwise irreconcilable. It causes the liberty of each to find not its limits, but its complement, the necessary condition of its continual existence--in the liberty of all.

"No man," says Michael Bakunin, "can recognize his own human worth, nor in consequence realize his full development, if he does not recognize the worth of his fellow men, and in co-operation with them, realize his own development through them. No man can emancipate himself, unless at the same time he emancipates those around him. My freedom is the freedom of all; for I am not really free--free not only in thought, but in deed--if my freedom and my right do not find their confirmation and sanction in the liberty and right of all men my equals.

"It matters much to me what all other men are, for however independent I may seem, or may believe myself to be, by virtue of my social position, whether as pope, czar, emperor, or prime minister, I am all the while the product of those who are the least among men. If these are ignorant, miserable, or enslaved, my existence is limited by their ignorance, misery, or slavery. I, though an intelligent and enlightened man, am made stupid by their stupidity; though brave, am enslaved by their slavery; though rich, tremble before their poverty; though privileged, grow pale at the thought of possible justice for them. I, who wish to be free, cannot be so, because around me are men who do not yet desire freedom, and, not desiring it, become, as opposed to me, the instruments of my oppression."

Solidarity, then, is the condition in which man can attain the highest degree of security and of well-being. Therefore, egoism itself, that is, the exclusive consideration of individual interests, impels man and human society towards solidarity. Or rather egoism and altruism (consideration of the interests of others) are united in this one sentiment, as the interest of the individual is one with the interests of society.

However, man could not pass at once from animalism to humanity; from brutal strife between man and man to the collective strife of all mankind, united in one brotherhood of mutual aid against external nature.

Guided by the advantages that association and the consequent division of labor offer, man evolved towards solidarity, but his evolution encountered an obstacle which led him, and still leads him, away from his aim. He discovered that he could realize the advantages of co-operation, at least up to a certain point, and for the material and primitive wants that then comprised all his needs, by making other men subject to himself, instead of associating on an equality with them. Thus the ferocious and anti-social instincts, inherited from his bestial ancestry, again obtained the upper hand. He forced the weaker to work for him, preferring to domineer over rather than to associate fraternally with his fellows. Perhaps also in most cases it was by exploiting the conquered in war that man learnt for the first time the benefits of association and the help that can be obtained from mutual support.

Thus it has come about that the establishment of the utility of co-operation, which ought to lead to the triumph of solidarity in all human concerns, has turned to the advantage of private property and of government; in other words, to the exploitation of the labor of the many, for the sake of the privileged few.

There has always been association and co-operation, without which human life would be impossible; but it has been co-operation imposed and regulated by the few in their own particular interest.

From this fact arises a great contradiction with which the history of mankind is filled. On the one hand, we find the tendency to associate and fraternize for the purpose of conquering and adapting the external world to human needs, and for the satisfaction of the human affections; while, on the other hand we see the tendency to divide into as many separate and hostile factions as there are different conditions of life. These factions are determined, for instance, by geographical and ethnological conditions, by differences in economic position, by privileges acquired by some and sought to be secured by others, or by suffering endured, with the ever recurring desire to rebel.

The principle of each for himself, that is, of war of all against all, has come in the course of time to complicate, lead astray, and paralyze the war of all combined against nature, for the common advantage of the human race, which could only be completely successful by acting on the principle of all for each, and each for all.

Great have been the evils which humanity has suffered by this intermingling of domination and exploitation with human association. But in spite of the atrocious oppression to which the masses submit, of the misery, vice, crime, and degradation which oppression and slavery produce, among the slaves and their masters, and in spite of the hatreds, the exterminating wars, and the antagonisms of artificially created interests, the social instinct has survived and even developed. Co-operation, having been always the necessary condition for successful combat against external nature, has therefore been the permanent cause of men's coming together, and consequently of the development of their sympathetic sentiments. Even the oppression of the masses has itself caused the oppressed to fraternize among themselves. Indeed it has been solely owing to this feeling of solidarity, more or less conscious and more or less widespread among the oppressed, that they have been able to endure the oppression, and that man has resisted the causes of death in his midst.

In the present, the immense development of production, the growth of human needs which cannot be satisfied except by the united efforts of a large number of men in all countries, the extended means of communication, habits of travel, science, literature, commerce, even war itself--all these have drawn and are still drawing humanity into a compact body, every section of which, closely knit together, can find its satisfaction and liberty only in the development and health of all other sections composing the whole.

The inhabitant of Naples is as much interested in the amelioration of the hygienic condition of the peoples on the banks of the Ganges, from whence the cholera is brought to him, as in the improvement of the sewerage of his own town. The well-being, liberty, or fortune of the mountaineer, lost among the precipices of the Appenines, does not depend alone on the state of well-being or of misery in which the inhabitants of his own village live, or even on the general condition of the Italian people, but also on the condition of the workers in America, or Australia, on the discovery of a Swedish scientist, on the moral and material conditions of the Chinese, on war or peace in Africa; in short, it depends on all the great and small circumstances which affect the human being in any spot whatever of the world.

In the present condition of society, the vast solidarity which unites all men is in a great degree unconscious, since it arises spontaneously from the friction of particular interests, while men occupy themselves little or not at all with general interests. And this is the most evident proof that solidarity is the natural law of human life, which imposes itself, so to speak, in spite of all obstacles, and even those artificially created by society as at present constituted.

On the other hand, the oppressed masses, never wholly resigned to oppression and misery, who today more than ever show themselves ardent for justice, liberty, and well-being, are beginning to understand that they cannot emancipate themselves except by uniting, through solidarity with all the oppressed and exploited over the whole world. And they understand also that the indispensable condition of their emancipation is the possession of the means of production, of the soil and of the instruments of labor, and further the abolition of private property. Science and the observation of social phenomena show that this abolition would be of immense advantage in the end, even to the privileged classes, if only they could bring themselves to renounce the spirit of domination, and concur with all their fellow men in laboring for the common good.

———————————

Now, should the oppressed masses some day refuse to work for their oppressors, should they take possession of the soil and the instruments of labor, and apply them for their own use and advantage, and that of all who work, should they no longer submit to the domination, either of brute force or economic privilege; should the spirit of human fellowship and the sentiment of human solidarity, strengthened by common interests, grow among the people, and put an end to strife between nations; then what ground would there be for the existence of a government?

Private property abolished, government--which is its defender --must disappear. Should it survive, it would continually tend to reconstruct, under one form or another, a privileged and oppressive class.

And the abolition of government does not, nor cannot, signify the doing away with human association.

Far otherwise, for that co-operation which today is enforced, and directed to the advantage of the few, would be free and voluntary, directed to the advantage of all. Therefore it would become more intense and efficacious.

The social instinct and the sentiment of solidarity would develop to the highest degree; and every individual would do all in his power for the good of others, as much for the satisfaction of his own well understood interests as for the gratification of his sympathetic sentiments.

By the free association of all, a social organization would arise through the spontaneous grouping of men according to their needs and sympathies, from the low to the high, from the simple to the complex, starting from the more immediate to arrive at the more distant and general interests. This organization would have for its aim the greatest good and fullest liberty to all; it would embrace all humanity in one common brotherhood, and would be modified and improved as circumstances were modified and changed, according to the teachings of experience.

This society of *free men*, this society of *friends* would be *Anarchy*.

II.

We have hitherto considered government as it is, and as it necessarily must be in a society founded upon privilege, upon the exploitation and oppression of man by man, upon antagonism of interests and social strife, in a word, upon private property.

We have seen how this state of strife, far from being a necessary condition of human life, is contrary to the interests of the individual and of the species. We have observed how co-operation, solidarity (of interest) is the law of human progress, and we have concluded that, with the abolition of private property and the cessation of all domination of man over man, there, would be no reason for government to exist--therefore it ought to be abolished.

But, it may be objected, if the principle on which social organization is now founded were to be changed, and solidarity substituted for strife, common property for private property, the government also would change its nature. Instead of being the protector and representative of the interests of one class, it would become, if there were no longer any classes, representative of all society. Its mission would be to secure and regulate social co-operation in the interests of all, and to fulfil public services of general utility. It would defend society against possible attempts to re-establish privilege, and prevent or repress all attacks, by whomsoever set on foot, against the life, well-being, or liberty of each.

There are in society certain matters too important, requiring too much constant, regular attention, for them to be left to the voluntary management of individuals, without danger of everything getting into disorder.

If there were no government, who would organize the supply and distribution of provisions? Who regulate matters pertaining to public hygiene, the postal, telegraph, and railway services, etc.? Who would direct public instruction? Who undertake those great works of exploration, improvement on a large scale, scientific enterprise, etc., which transform the face of the earth and augment a hundredfold the power of man?

Who would care for the preservation and increase of capital, that it might be transmitted to posterity, enriched and improved?

Who would prevent the destruction of the forests, or the irrational exploitation, and therefore impoverishment of the soil?

Who would there be to prevent and repress crimes, that is, anti-social acts?

What of those who, disregarding the law of solidarity, would not work? Or of those who might spread infectious disease in a country, by refusing to submit to the regulation of hygiene by science? Or what again could be done with those who, whether insane or no, might set fire to the harvest, injure children, or abuse and take advantage of the weak?

To destroy private property and abolish existing government, without reconstituting a government that would organize collective life and secure social solidarity, would not be to abolish privilege, and bring peace and prosperity upon earth. It would be to destroy, every social bond, to leave humanity to fall back into barbarism, to begin again the reign of "each for himself;" which would establish the triumph, firstly, of brute force, and, secondly, of economic privilege.

Such are the objections brought forward by authoritarians, even by those who are Socialists, that is, who wish to abolish private property, and class government founded upon the system of private property.

We reply:

In the first place, it is not true that with a change of social conditions, the nature of the government and its functions would also change. Organs and functions are inseparable terms. Take from an organ its function, and either the organ will die, or the function will reinstate itself. Place an army in a country where there is no reason for or fear of foreign war, and this army will provoke war, or, if it do not succeed in doing that, it will disband. A police force, where there are no crimes to discover, and delinquents to arrest, will provoke or invent crimes, or will cease to exist.

For centuries, there existed in France an institution, now included in the administration of the forests, for the extermination of the wolves and other noxious beasts. No one will be surprised to learn that, just on account of this institution, wolves still exist in France, and that, in rigorous seasons, they do great damage. The public take little heed of the wolves, because there are the appointed officials, whose duty it is to think about them. And the officials do hunt them, but in an *intelligent* manner, sparing their caves, and allowing time for reproduction, that they may not run the risk of entirely destroying such an *interesting* species. The French peasants have indeed little confidence in these official wolf-hunters, and regard them rather as the wolf-preservers. And, of course, what would these officials do if there were no longer any wolves to exterminate?

A government, that is, a number of persons deputed to make the laws, and entitled to use the collective forces of society to make every individual to respect these laws, already constitutes a class privileged and separated from the rest of the community. Such a class, like every elected body, will seek instinctively to. enlarge its powers; to place itself above the control of the people; to impose its tendencies, and to make its own interests predominate. Placed in a privileged position, the government always finds itself in antagonism to the masses, of whose force it disposes.

Furthermore, a government, with the best intention, could never satisfy everybody, even if it succeeded in satisfying some. It must therefore always be defending itself against the discontented, and for that reason must ally itself with the satisfied section of the community for necessary support. And in this manner will arise again the old story of a privileged class, which cannot help but be developed in conjunction with the government. This class, if it could not again acquire possession of the soil, would certainly monopolize the most favored spots, and would not be in the end less oppressive, or less an instrument of exploitation than the capitalist class.

The governors, accustomed to command, would never wish to mix with the common crowd. If they could not retain the power in their own hands, they would at least secure to themselves privileged positions for the time when they would be out of office. They would use all the means they have in their power to get their own friends elected as their successors, who would in their turn be supported and protected by their predecessors. And thus the government would pass and repass into the same hands, and the *democracy*, that is, the government presumably of the whole people, would end, as it always has done, in becoming an *oligarchy*, or the government of a few, the government of a class.

And this all-powerful, oppressive, all-absorbing oligarchy would have always in its care, that is, at its disposition, every bit of social capital, all public services, from the production and distribution of provisions to the manufacture of matches, from the control of the university to that of the music hall.

But let us even suppose that the government did not necessarily constitute a privileged class, and could exist without forming around itself a new privileged class. Let us imagine that it could remain truly representative, the servant--if you will--of all society. What purpose would it then serve? In what particular and in what manner would it augment the power, intelligence, spirit of solidarity, care of the general welfare, present and to come, that at any given moment existed in a given society?

It is always the old story of the man with bound limbs, who, having managed to live in spite of his bands, believes that he lives by means of them. We are accustomed to live under a government, which makes use of all that energy, that intelligence, and that will which it can direct to its own ends; but which hinders, paralyzes and suppresses those that are useless or hostile to it. And we imagine that all that is done in society is done by virtue of the government, and that without the government there would be neither energy, intelligence, nor good will in society. So it happens (as we have already said) that the proprietor who has possessed himself of the soil, has it cultivated for his own particular profit, leaving the laborer the barest necessities of life for which he can and will continue to labor. While the enslaved laborer thinks that he could not live without his master, as though it were *he* who created the earth and the forces of nature.

What can government of itself add to the moral and material forces which exist in a society? Unless it be like the God of the Bible, who created the universe out of nothing?

As nothing is created in the so-called material world, so in this more complicated form of the material world, which is the social world, nothing can be created. And therefore governors can dispose of no other force than that which is already in society. And indeed not by any means of all of that, as much force is necessarily paralyzed and destroyed by governmental methods of action, while more again is wasted in the friction with rebellious elements, inevitably great in such an artificial mechanism. Whenever governors originate anything of themselves, it is as men and not as governors, that they do so. And of that amount of force, both material and moral, which does remain at the disposition of the government, only an infinitesimally small part achieves an end really useful to society. The remainder is either consumed in actively repressing rebellious opposition, or is otherwise diverted from the aim of general utility, and turned to the profit of the few, and to the injury of the majority of men.

So much has been made of the part that individual initiative and social action play respectively in the life and progress of human society; and such is the confusion of metaphysical language, that those who affirm that individual initiative is the source and agency of all action seem to be asserting something quite preposterous. In reality, it is a truism, which becomes apparent directly we begin to explain the actual facts represented by these words.

The real being is the man, the individual; society or the collectivity, and the State or government which professes to represent it, if not hollow abstractions, can be nothing else than aggregates of individuals. And it is within the individual organism that all thoughts and all human action necessarily have their origin. Originally individual, they become collective thoughts and actions, when shared in common by many individuals. Social action, then, is not the negation, nor the complement of individual initiative, but it is the sum total of the initiatives, thoughts and actions of all the individuals composing society: a result which, other things equal, is more or less great according as the individual forces tend toward the same aim, or are divergent and opposed. If, on the other hand, as the authoritarians make out, by social action is meant governmental action, then it is again the result of individual forces, but only of those individuals who either form part of the government, or by virtue of their position are enabled to influence the conduct of the government.

Thus, in the contest of centuries between liberty and authority, or, in other words, between social equality and social castes, the question at issue has not really been the relations between society and the individual, nor the increase of individual independence at the cost of social control, or *vice versa*. Rather it has had to do with preventing any one individual from oppressing the others; with giving to everyone the same rights and the same means of action. It has had to do with substituting the initiative of all, which must naturally result in the advantage of all, for the initiative of the few, which necessarily results in the suppression of all the others. It is always, in short, the question of putting an end to the domination and exploitation of man by man in such a way that all are interested in the common welfare; and that the individual force of each, instead of oppressing, combating or suppressing others, will find the possibility of complete development, and every one will seek to associate with others for the greater advantage of all.

From what we have said, it follows that the existence of a government, even upon the hypothesis that the ideal government of authoritarian Socialists were possible, far from producing an increase of productive force, would immensely diminish it; because the government would restrict initiative to the few. It would give these few the right to do all things, without being able, of course, to endow them with the knowledge or understanding of all things.

In fact, if you divest legislation and all the operations of government of what is intended to protect the privileged, and what represents the wishes of the privileged classes alone, nothing remains but the aggregate of individual governors. "The State," says Sismondi, "is always a conservative power that authorizes, regulates and organizes the conquests of progress (and history testifies that it applies them to the profit of its own and the other privileged classes) but never does inaugurate them. New ideas always originate from beneath, are conceived in the foundations of society, and then, when divulged, they become opinion and grow. But they must always meet on their path, and combat the constituted powers of tradition, custom, privilege and error."

In order to understand how society could exist without a government, it is sufficient to turn our attention for a short space to what actually goes on in our present society. We shall see that in reality the most important social functions are fulfilled even now-a-days outside the intervention of government. Also that government only interferes to exploit the masses, or defend the privileged class, or, lastly, to sanction, most unnecessarily, all that has been done without its aid, often in spite of and in opposition to it. Men work, exchange, study, travel, follow as they choose the current rules of morality, or hygiene; they profit by the progress of science and art, have numberless mutual interests without ever feeling the need of anyone to direct them how to conduct themselves in regard to these matters. On the contrary, it is just those things in which there is no governmental interference that prosper best, and that give rise to the least contention, being unconsciously adapted to the wish of all in the way found most useful and agreeable.

Nor is government more necessary in the case of large undertakings, or for those public services which require the constant co-operation of many people of different conditions and countries. Thousands of these undertakings are even now the work of voluntarily formed associations. And these are, by the acknowledgment of every one, the undertakings which succeed the best. Nor do we refer to the association of capitalists, organized by means of exploitation, although even they show capabilities and powers of free association, which may extend *ad libitum* until it embraces all the peoples of all lands, and includes the widest and most varying interests. But we speak rather of those associations inspired by the love of humanity, or by the passion for knowledge, or even simply by the desire for amusement and love of applause, as these better represent such grouping as will exist in a society where, private property and internal strife between men being abolished, each will find his interests synonymous with the interests of every one else, and his greatest satisfaction in doing good and pleasing others. Scientific societies and congresses, international life-boat and Red Cross associations, etc., laborers' unions, peace societies, volunteers who hasten to the rescue at times of great public calamity are all examples, among thousands, of that power of the spirit of association, which always shows itself when a need arises, or an enthusiasm takes hold, and the means do not fail. That voluntary associations do not cover the world, and do not embrace every branch of material and moral activity, is the fault of the obstacles placed in their way by governments, of the antagonisms created by the possession of private property, and of the impotence and degradation to which the monopolizing of wealth on the part of the few reduces the majority of mankind.

The government takes charge, for instance, of the postal and telegraphic services. But in what way does it really assist them? When the people are in such a condition as to be able to enjoy, and feel the need of such services, they will think about organizing them; and the man with the necessary technical knowledge will not require a certificate from the government to enable him to set to work. The more general and urgent the need, the more volunteers will offer to satisfy it. Would the people have the ability necessary to provide and distribute provisions? Oh! never fear, they will not die of hunger, waiting for a government to pass laws on the subject. Wherever a government exists, it must wait until the people have first organized everything, and then come with its laws to sanction and exploit that which has been already done. It is evident that private interest is the great motive for all activity. That being so, when the interest of every one becomes the interest of each (and it necessarily will become so as soon as private property is abolished) then all will be active. And if now they work in the interest of the few, so much the more and so much the better will they work to satisfy the interests of all. It is hard to understand how anyone can believe that public services indispensable to social life can be better secured by order of a government than through the workers themselves, who by their own choice or by agreement made with others, carry them out under the immediate control of all interested.

Certainly in every collective undertaking on a large scale, there is need for division of labor, for technical direction, administration, etc. But the authoritarians are merely playing with words, when they deduce a reason for the existence of government, from the very real necessity for organization of labor. The government, we must repeat, is the aggregate of the individuals who have had given them, or have taken the right or the means to make laws, and force the people to obey them. The administrators, engineers, etc., on the other hand, are men who receive or assume the charge of doing a certain work, and who do it. Government signifies delegation of power, that is, abdication of the initiative and sovereignty of every one into the hands of the few. Administration signifies delegation of work, that is, a charge given and accepted, the free exchange of services founded on free agreement.

A governor is a privileged person, because he has the right to command others, and to avail himself of the force of others, to make his own ideas and desires triumph. An administrator or technical director is a worker like others, in a society, of course, where all have equal opportunities of development, and all are, or can be, at the same time intellectual and manual workers; when there are no other differences between men than those derived from diversity of talents, and all work and all social functions give an equal right to the enjoyment of social advantages. The functions of government are, in short, not to be confounded with administrative functions, as they are essentially different. That they are today so often confused is entirely on account of the existence of economic and political privilege.

But let us hasten to pass on to those functions for which government is thought indispensable by all who are not Anarchists. These are the internal and external defence of society, that is, War, Police and Justice.

Government being abolished, and social wealth at the disposal of every one, all antagonism between various nations would soon cease; and there would consequently be no more cause for war. Moreover, in the present state of the world, in any country where the spirit of rebellion is growing, even if it do not find an echo throughout the land, it will be certain of so much sympathy that the government will not dare to send all its troops to a foreign war, for fear the revolution should break out at home. But even supposing that the rulers of countries not yet emancipated would wish and could attempt to reduce a free people to servitude, would these require a government to enable them to defend themselves? To make war, we need men who have the necessary geographical and technical knowledge, and, above all, people willing to fight. A government has no means of augmenting the ability of the former, or the willingness or courage of the latter. And the experience of history teaches that a people really desirous of defending their own country are invincible. In Italy every one knows how thrones tremble, and regular armies of hired soldiers vanish before troops of volunteers, that is, armies Anarchically formed.

And as to the police and justice, many imagine that if it were not for the police and the judges, everybody would be free to kill, violate or injure others as the humor took him; that Anarchists, if they are true to their principles, would like to see this strange kind of liberty respected; "liberty" that violates or destroys the life and freedom of others unrestrained. Such people believe that we, having overthrown the government and private property, shall then tranquilly allow the re-establishment of both, out of respect for the "liberty" of those who may feel the need of having a government and private property. A strange mode indeed of construing our ideas! In truth, one may better answer such notions with a shrug of the shoulders than by taking the trouble to confute them.

The liberty we wish for, for ourselves and others, is not an absolute, abstract, metaphysical liberty, which in practice can only amount to the oppression of the weak. But we wish for a tangible liberty, the possible liberty, which is the conscious communion of interests, that is, voluntary solidarity. We proclaim the maxim: *Do as you will;* and in this our program is almost entirely contained, because, as may be easily understood, we hold that in a society without government or property, each one *will wish that which he should.*

But if, in consequence of a false education, received in the present society, or of physical disease, or whatever other cause, an individual should wish to injure others, you may be sure we should adopt all the means in our power to prevent him. As we know that a man's character is the consequence of his physical organism, and of the cosmic and social influences surrounding him, we certainly shall not confound the sacred right of self-defence, with the absurdly assumed right to punish. Also, we shall not regard the delinquent, that is, the man who commits anti-social acts, as the rebel he seems in the eyes of the judges nowadays. We shall regard him as a sick brother in need of cure. We therefore shall not act towards him in the spirit of hatred, when repressing him, but shall confine ourselves solely to self-protection. We shall not seek to revenge ourselves, but rather to rescue the unfortunate one by every means that science suggests. In theory, Anarchists may go astray like others, losing sight of the reality under a semblance of logic; but it is quite certain that the emancipated people will not let their dearly bought liberty and welfare be attacked with impunity. If the necessity arose, they would provide for their own defence against the anti-social tendencies of certain amongst them. But how do those whose business it now is to make the laws, protect society? Or those others who live by seeking for and inventing new infringements of law? Even now, when the masses of the people really disapprove of anything and think it injurious, they always find a way to prevent it very much more effectually than all the professional legislators, constables or judges. During insurrections, the people, though very mistakenly, have enforced the respect for private property; and they have secured this respect far better than an army of policemen could have done.

Customs always follow the needs and sentiments of the majority; and they are always the more respected, the less they are subject to the sanction of law. This is because every one sees and comprehends their utility, and because the interested parties, not deluding themselves with the idea that government will protect them, are themselves concerned in seeing the custom respected. The economical use of water is of very great importance to a caravan crossing the deserts of Africa. Under these circumstances, water is a sacred thing; and no sane man dreams of wasting it. Conspirators are obliged to act secretly; so secrecy is preserved among them, and obloquy rests on whosoever violates it. Gambling debts are not guaranteed by law; but among gamblers it is considered dishonorable not to pay them, and the delinquent feels himself dishonored by not fulfilling his obligations.

Is it on account of the police that more people are not murdered? The greater part of the Italian people never see the police except at long intervals. Millions of men go over the mountains and through the country, far from the protecting eye of authority, where they might be attacked without the slightest fear of their assailants being traced; but they run no greater risk than those who live in the best guarded spots. Statistics show that the number of crimes rise in proportion to the increase of repressive measures; while they vary rapidly with the fluctuations of economic conditions and with the state of public opinion.

Preventive laws, however, only concern unusual, exceptional acts. Every-day life goes on beyond the limits of the criminal code, and is regulated almost unconsciously by the tacit and voluntary assent of all, by means of a number of usages and customs much more important to social life than the dictates of law. And they are also much better observed, although completely divested of any sanction beyond the natural odium which falls upon those who violate them, and such injury as this odium brings with it.

When disputes arise, would not voluntarily accepted arbitration or the pressure of public opinion be far more likely to bring about a just settlement of the difficulties in question than an irresponsible magistrate, who has the right to pass judgment upon everybody and everything, and who is necessarily incompetent and therefore unjust?

As every form of government only serves to protect the privileged classes, so do police and judges only aim at repressing those crimes, often not considered criminal by the masses, which offend only the privileges of the rulers or property-owners. For the real defence of society, the defence of the welfare and liberty of all, there can be nothing more pernicious than the formation of this class of functionaries, who exist on the pretence of defending all, and therefore habitually regard every man as game to be hunted down, often striking at the command of a superior officer, without themselves even knowing why, like hired assassins and mercenaries.

All that you have said may be true, say some; Anarchy may be a perfect form of social life; but we have no desire to take a leap in the dark. Therefore, tell us how your society will be organized. Then follows a long string of questions, which would be very interesting if it were our business to study the problems that might arise in an emancipated society, but of which it is useless and absurd to imagine that we could now offer a definite solution. According to what method will children be taught? How will production and distribution be organized? Will there still be large cities, or will people spread equally over all the surface of the earth? Will all the inhabitants of Siberia winter at Nice? Will every one dine on partridges and drink champagne? Who will be the miners and sailors? Who will clear the drains? Will the sick be nursed at home or in hospitals? Who will arrange the railway time-table? What will happen if the engine-driver falls ill while the train is on its way? And so on, without end, as though we could prophesy all the knowledge and experience of the future time, or could, in the name of Anarchy, prescribe for the coming man what time he should go to bed, and on what days he should cut his nails!

Indeed if our readers expect from us an answer to these questions, or even to those among them really serious and important, which cannot be anything more than our own private opinion at this present hour, we must have succeeded badly in our endeavor to explain what Anarchy is.

We are no more prophets than other men; and should we pretend to give an official solution to all the problems that will arise in the life of the future society, we should have indeed a curious idea of the abolition of government. We should then be describing a government, dictating, like the clergy, a universal code for the present and all future time. Seeing that we have neither police nor prisons to enforce our doctrine, humanity might laugh with impunity at us and our pretensions.

Nevertheless, we consider seriously all the problems of social life which now suggest themselves, on account of their scientific interest, and because, hoping to see Anarchy realized, we wish to help towards the organization of the new society. We have therefore our own ideas on these subjects, ideas which are to our minds likely to be permanent or transitory, according to the respective cases. And did space permit, we might add somewhat more on these points. But the fact that we today think in a certain way on a given question is no proof that such will be the mode of procedure in the future. Who can foresee the activities which may develop in humanity when it is emancipated from misery and oppression? When all have the means of instruction and self-development? When the strife between men, with the hatred and rancour it breeds, will be no longer a necessary condition of existence? Who can foresee the progress of science, the new sources of production, means of communication, etc.?

The one essential is that a society be constituted in which the exploitation and domination of man by man are impossible. That the society, in other words, be such that the means of existence and development of labor be free and open to every one, and all be able to co-operate, according to their wishes and their knowledge, in the organization of social life. Under such conditions, everything will necessarily be performed in compliance with the needs of all, according to the knowledge and possibilities of the moment. And everything will improve with the increase of knowledge and power.

In fact, a program which would touch the basis of the new social constitution could not do more, after all, than indicate a method. And method, more than anything else, defines parties and determines their importance in history. Method apart, every one says he wishes for the good of mankind; and many do truly wish for it. As parties disappear, every organized action directed to a definite end disappears likewise. It is therefore necessary to consider Anarchy as, above all, a method.

There are two methods by which the different parties, not Anarchistic, expect, or say they expect, to bring about the greatest good of each and all. These are the authoritarian or State Socialist and the individualist methods. The former entrusts the direction of social life to a few; and it would result in the exploitation and oppression of the masses by that few. The second party trusts to the free initiative of individuals, and proclaims, if not the abolition, the reduction of government. However, as it respects private property, and is founded on the principle of each for himself, and therefore on competition, its liberty is only the liberty of the strong, the license of those who have, to oppress and exploit the weak who have nothing. Far from producing harmony, it would tend always to augment the distance between the rich and the poor, and end also through exploitation and domination in authority. This second method, Individualism, is in theory a kind of Anarchy without Socialism. It is therefore no better than a lie, because liberty is not possible without equality, and true Anarchy cannot be without Solidarity, without Socialism. The criticism which Individualists pass on government is merely the wish to deprive it of certain functions, to virtually hand them over to the capitalist. But it cannot attack those repressive functions which form the essence of government; for without an armed force the proprietary system could not be upheld. Nay, even more, under Individualism, the repressive power of government must always increase, in proportion to the increase, by means of free competition, of the want of equality and harmony.

Anarchists present a new method; the free initiative of all and free agreement; then, after the revolutionary abolition of private property, every one will have equal power to dispose of social wealth. This method, not admitting the re-establishment of private property, must lead, by means of free association, to the complete triumph of the principles of solidarity.

Thus we see that all the problems put forward to combat the Anarchistic idea are on the contrary arguments in favor of Anarchy; because it alone indicates the way in which, by experience, those solutions which correspond to the dicta of science, and to the needs and wishes of all, can best be found.

How will children be educated? We do not know. What then? The parents, teachers and all who are interested in the progress of the rising generation, will meet, discuss, agree and differ, and then divide according to their various opinions, putting into practice the methods which they respectively hold to be best. That method which, when tried, produces the best results, will triumph in the end.

And so for all the problems that may arise.

According to what we have so far said, it is evident that Anarchy, as the Anarchists conceive it, and as alone it can be comprehended, is based on Socialism. Furthermore, were it not for that school of Socialists who artificially divide the natural unity of the social question, considering only some detached points, and were it not also for the equivocations with which they strive to hinder the social revolution, we might say right away that Anarchy is synonymous with Socialism. Because both signify the abolition of exploitation and of the domination of man over man, whether maintained by the force of arms or by the monopolization of the means of life.

Anarchy, like Socialism, has for its basis and necessary point of departure *equality of conditions*. Its aim is *solidarity*, and its method *liberty*. It is not perfection, nor is it the absolute ideal, which, like the horizon, always recedes as we advance towards it. But it is the open road to all progress and to all improvement, made in the interest of all humanity.

There are authoritarians who grant that Anarchy is the mode of social life which alone opens the way to the attainment of the highest possible good for mankind, because it alone can put an end to every class interested in keeping the masses oppressed and miserable. They also grant that Anarchy is possible, because it does nothing more than release humanity from an obstacle--government--against which it has always had to fight its painful way towards progress. Nevertheless, these authoritarians, reinforced by many warm lovers of liberty and justice in theory, retire into their last entrenchments, because they are afraid of liberty, and cannot be persuaded that mankind could live and prosper without teachers and pastors; still, hard pressed by the truth, they pitifully demand to have the reign of liberty put off for a while, indeed for as long as possible.

Such is the substance of the arguments that meet us at this stage.

A society without a government, which would act by free, voluntary co-operation, trusting entirely to the spontaneous action of those interested, and founded altogether on solidarity and sympathy, is certainly, they say, a very beautiful ideal, but, like all ideals, it is a castle in the air. We find ourselves placed in a human society, which has always been divided into oppressors and oppressed; and if the former are full of the spirit of domination, and have all the vices of tyrants, the latter are corrupted by servility, and have those still worse vices, which are the result of enslavement. The sentiment of solidarity is far from being dominant in man at the present day; and if it is true that the different classes of men are becoming more and more unanimous among themselves, it is none the less true that that which is most conspicuous and impresses itself most on human character today is the struggle for existence. It is a fact that each fights daily against every one else, and competition presses upon all, workmen and masters, causing every man to become a wolf towards every other man. How can these men, educated in a society based upon antagonism between individuals as well as classes, be transformed in a moment and become capable of living in a society in which each shall do as he likes, and as he should, without external coercion, caring for the good of others, simply by the impulse of their own nature? And with what heart or what common sense can you trust to a revolution on the part of an ignorant, turbulent mass, weakened by misery, stupefied by priestcraft, who are today blindly sanguinary and tomorrow will let themselves be humbugged by any knave, who dares to call himself their master? Would it not be more prudent to advance gradually towards the Anarchistic ideal, passing through Republican, Democratic and Socialistic stages? Will not an educative government, composed of the best men, be necessary to prepare the advancing generations for their future destiny?

These objections also ought not to appear valid if we have succeeded in making our readers understand what we have already said, and in convincing them of it. But in any case, even at the risk of repetition, it may be as well to answer them.

We find ourselves continually met by the false notion that government is in itself a new force, sprung up one knows not whence, which of itself adds something to the sum of the force and capability of those whom it is composed and of those who obey it. While, on the contrary, all that is done is done by individual men. The government, as a government, adds nothing save the tendency to monopolize for the advantage of certain parties or classes, and to repress all initiative from beyond its own circle.

To abolish authority or government does not mean to destroy the individual or collective forces, which are at work in society, nor the influence men exert over one another. That would be to reduce humanity to an aggregate of inert and separate atoms; an impossibility which, if it could be performed, would be the destruction of any society, the death blow to mankind. To abolish authority, means to abolish the monopoly of force and of influence. It means to abolish that state of things by which social force, that is, the collective force of all in a society, is made the instrument of the thought, will and interests of a small number of individuals. These, by means of the collective force, suppress the liberty of every one else, to the advantage of their own ideas. In other words, it means to destroy a mode of organization by means of which the future is exploited, between one revolution and another, to the profit of those who have been the victors of the moment.

Michael Bakunin, in an article published in 1872, asserts that the great means of action of the International were the propagating of their ideas, and the organization of the spontaneous action of its members in regard to the masses. He then adds:

"To whoever might pretend that action so organized would be an outrage on the liberty of the masses, or an attempt to create a new authoritative power, we would reply that he is a sophist and a fool. So much the worse for those who ignore the natural, social law of human solidarity, to the extent of imagining that an absolute mutual independence of individuals and of masses is a possible or even desirable thing. To desire it, would be to wish for the destruction of society; for all social life is nothing else than this mutual and incessant interdependence among individuals and masses. All individuals, even the most gifted and strongest, indeed most of all the most gifted and strongest, are at every moment of their lives, at the same time, producers and products. Equal liberty for every individual is only the resultant, continually reproduced, of this mass of material, intellectual and moral influence exercised on him by all the individuals around him, belonging to the society in which he was born, has developed and dies. To wish to escape this influence in the name of a transcendental liberty, divine, absolutely egoistic and sufficient to itself, is the tendency to annihilation. To refrain from influencing others, would mean to refrain from all social action, indeed to abstain from all expression of one's thoughts and sentiments, and simply to become non-existent. This independence, so much extolled by idealists and metaphysicians, individual liberty conceived in this sense would amount to self-annihilation.

"In nature, as in human society, which is also a part of this same nature, all that exists lives only by complying with the supreme conditions of interaction, which is more or less positive and potent with regard to the lives of other beings, according to the nature of the individual. And when we vindicate the liberty of the masses, we do not pretend to abolish anything of the natural influences that individuals or groups of individuals exert upon one another. What we wish for is the abolition of artificial influences, which are privileged, legal and official."

Certainly, in the present state of mankind, oppressed by misery, stupefied by superstition and sunk in degradation, the human lot depends upon a relatively small number of individuals. Of course, all men will not be able to rise in a moment to the height of perceiving their duty, or even the enjoyment of so regulating their own action that others also will derive the greatest possible benefit from it. But because nowadays the thoughtful and guiding forces at work in society are few, that is no reason for paralyzing them still more, and for the subjection of many individuals to the direction of a few. It is no reason for constituting society in such a manner that the most active forces, the highest capacities are, in the end, found outside the government, and almost deprived of influence on social life. All this now happens owing to the inertia that secured positions foster, to heredity, to protectionism, to party spirit and to all the mechanism of government. For those in government office, taken out of their former social position, primarily concerned in retaining power, lose all power to act spontaneously, and become only an obstacle to the free action of others.

With the abolition of this negative potency constituting government, society will become that which it can be, with the given forces and capabilities of the moment. If there are educated men desirous of spreading education, they will organize the schools, and will be constrained to make the use and enjoyment to be derived from education felt. And if there are no such men, or only a few of them, a government cannot create them. All it can do, as in fact it does nowadays, is to take these few away from practical, fruitful work in the sphere of education, and put them to direct from above what has to be imposed by the help of a police system. So they make out of intelligent and impassionate teachers mere politicians, who become useless parasites, entirely absorbed in imposing their own hobbies, and in maintaining themselves in power.

If there are doctors and teachers of hygiene, they will organize themselves for the service of health. And if there are none, a government cannot create them; all that it can do is to discredit them in the eyes of the people, who are inclined to entertain suspicions, sometimes only too well founded, with regard to everything which is imposed upon them.

If there are engineers and mechanics, they will organize the railways, etc; and if there are none, a government cannot create them.

The revolution, by abolishing government and private property, will not create force which does not exist; but it will leave a free field for the exercise of all available force and of all existent capacity. While it will destroy every class interested in keeping the masses degraded, it will act in such a way that every one will be free to work and make his influence felt, in proportion to his own capacity, and in conformity with his sentiments and interests. And it is only thus that the elevation of the masses is possible; for it is only with liberty that one can learn to be free, as it is only by working that one can learn to work. A government, even had it no other advantages, must always have that of habituating the governed to subjection, and must also tend to become more oppressive and more necessary, in proportion as its subjects are more obedient and docile.

But suppose government were the direction of affairs by the best people. Who are the best? And how shall we recognize their superiority. The majority are generally attached to old prejudices, and have ideas and instincts already outgrown by the more favored minority. But of the various minorities, who all believe themselves in the right, as no doubt many of them are in part, which shall be chosen to rule? And by whom? And by what criterion? Seeing that the future alone can prove which among them is the most superior. If you choose a hundred partisans of dictatorship, you will discover that each one of the hundred believes himself capable of being, if not sole dictator, at least of assisting very materially in the dictatorial government. The dictators would be those who, by one means or another, succeeded in imposing themselves on society. And, in course of time, all their energy would inevitably be employed in defending themselves against the attacks of their adversaries, totally oblivious of their desire, if ever they had had it, to be merely an educative power.

Should government be, on the other hand, elected by universal suffrage, and so be the emanation, more or less sincere, of the wish of the majority? But if you consider these worthy electors as incapable of providing for their own interests, how can they ever be capable of themselves choosing directors to guide them wisely? How solve this problem of social alchemy: To elect a government of geniuses by the votes of a mass of fools? And what will be the lot of the minority, who are the most intelligent, most active and most advanced in society?

To solve the social problem to the advantage of all, there is only one way. To expel the government by revolutionary means, to expropriate the holders of social wealth, putting everything at the disposition of all, and to leave all existing force, capacity and good-will among men free to provide for the needs of all.

We fight for Anarchy and for Socialism; because we believe that Anarchy and Socialism ought to be brought into operation as soon as possible. Which means that the revolution must drive away the government, abolish private property, and entrust all public service, which will then embrace all social life, to the spontaneous, free, unofficial and unauthorized operation of all those interested and all those willing volunteers.

There will certainly be difficulties and inconveniences; but the people will be resolute; and they alone can solve all difficulties Anarchically, that is, by direct action of those interested and by free agreement.

We cannot say whether Anarchy and Socialism will triumph after the next revolutionary attempt; but this is certain, that if any of the so-called transition programs triumph, it will be because we have been temporarily beaten, and never because we have thought it wise to leave in existence any one part of that evil system under which humanity groans.

Whatever happens, we shall have some influence on events, by our numbers, our energy, our intelligence and our steadfastness. Also, even if we are now conquered, our work will not have been in vain; for the more decided we shall have been in aiming at the realization of all our demands, the less there will be of government and of private property in the new society. And we shall have done a great work; for human progress is measured by the degree in which government and private property are administered.

If today we fall without lowering our colors, our cause is certain of victory tomorrow.

Printed in Great Britain
by Amazon